Leavings

Leavings

Poems by

Stephanie Kay Sugioka

Cover design by Shay Culligan
Cover image by Teslariu Mihai on Unsplash
Author photo by Sarah G. Richards

ISBN: 979-8-90146-725-1
Library of Congress Control Number: 2026935820

Kelsay Books
502 South 1040 East, A-119
American Fork, Utah 84003
Kelsaybooks.com

For Aaron and Sarah

Acknowledgments

Thanks are due to the editors of the following publications:

The Beloit Poetry Journal: "After Reading *The Tale of Genji*"

Calyx: "Surroundings," "A Commuter in Wisconsin"

Festschrift for Elliott Coleman: "Birds"

The Forbidden Stitch: An Asian American Women's Anthology (Calyx Books): "Legacy"

The Sow's Ear: "For a Young Son in Autumn," "Marriage," "Father of Waters," "Van Gogh in a Form of Limitation"

I am especially indebted to Eleanor Wilner for editing and helping me place my poems in order.

Contents

V. A Form of Limitation

I.
What Is Left

Husks

Before you begin
to read these words
I must warn you
that they are not
the thing itself—
only leavings,
husks,
hollow as cicada shells.

The real thing, it seems,
is always somewhere else.
It's as if you were to pull away,
one at a time,
the petals of a rose.
You see—what is left,
after the last petal is gone—
this is what I wanted to tell you.

After Reading *The Tale of Genji*

In ancient Japan the ladies
draped their souls out of the windows
in silks of acacia yellow, plum blossom red,
wisteria blue, and the ivory of chrysanthemums
that have faded to perfection.
The ladies themselves were hidden
behind blinds, behind screens, behind fans.
And when the silks were folded into their boxes
it was impossible to know
which soul belonged to which woman.

For a woman's soul is like wind
and may only be known by
what it touches
(and so you see I lied—
it was not their souls at all
but only wind-rippled silk).
The men riding by on their horses
were, however, impressed.

In ancient Japan a sword was judged
by how precisely it might sever a flower
without disturbing the plant
from which the flower came.

Once there was a river with no bridge.
On one side, screened by bamboo,
there walked a lady with a flower,
on the other a man with a sword.
But his horse would not cross the water
and disgusted he threw his sword into the river.

For a woman's soul is like water.
It is futile to try to slice it
with even the finest of swords.

In ancient Japan the man
would throw the image of his beloved
into the river
hoping the gods would find it
and deliver her to him.
But the water would wear the image smooth
by the time it had reached the gods
and so the gods were confused
as to who was the beloved.

At the bottom of the river
a sword lies rusting
and over the river the willows hang
like grieving ladies-in-waiting.
For a woman's soul is like water
and may only be known
by a drowning.

Surroundings

> *To the one who overcomes . . . I will give a white stone, and on it a new name written, which no one knows but the one who receives it.*
>
> —Revelation 2:17

Here where the shapes of the mountains
are vague enough to form the body of night
I am almost contained.
The wood of the swinging bridge
is the fragile splintered silver of bone.
Beneath, the river rushes
in this deep vein of the mountains.

On either side of the path to the cabin
the cricket voices rise and fall—
bright bits of sound
in two great gourds
that shake as if in answer
to one another.
The quaver of the screech owl's call
is a tin cup filling slowly
with black water.

By the dingy lamplight of the cabin
the strands of my work are almost golden.
With my hook I catch the thread
joining each stitch to the other
forming an open, a spiderweb, pattern—
an exercise in containing emptiness.
Or, if you will, I've left places
for the dark ragged breath of God
to blow through.

There are spaces also in my body
that I feel as I lie in the mildewed bed.
I am waiting for a word.
Perhaps it will be a name.
It will be as silent as
the O of a fish's mouth.
It will be a white stone
dropping quickly
through dark water.

Legacy

This is the eldest daughter
of wind and of wood.
Her words are as irrelevant
and as lost
as the broken song
of wind and bamboo.
The boys,
only three and five,
are unaware that I
am a species of ghost
in this their high glass house.
(The older one still insists
his mother must be mine.)
So when I arrive
they run figure eights around me,
triumphantly announcing
that I am there
(and, gullible as always,
I believe them).
This is the eldest daughter.
A small sound gnaws at her sleep,
a tedious, uneasy creaking
of pine branches
crossed
against one another.
Today, for some reason,
my father and stepmother
want to discuss their wills.
It is understood that the boys
should inherit the house.

Of an oriental design,
made to let in as much light
as the dogwoods, maples, and oaks
will allow,
it manages, somehow,
to look like an airport.
This is the house
that sprang phoenix-like
from the ruins of the former,
(my other) family.
(I've never lived there myself.)
          This is the eldest daughter.
          Music pierces her skull
          like twirling needles.
          It is the Japanese flutes
          that sing the panicked movement
          of her hands
          like broken-winged birds.
We finish our discussion
with a wicked stepmother joke,
and I take my leave.
Then out with the boys
to the rock garden
to learn who has watered
which crocus.
And they shall inherit
a house of light.
I believe in their small round lives
as I believe
in the round white stones
at our feet.

This is the eldest daughter
of wind and of wood.
Her legacy is a house
where no light shines.
The reeds sing it
whispery lullabies,
and hemlocks stroke
its splintered sides.
She is the black wind
that haunts the house—
rushing, always rushing
out of the room
down the hall
around the corner
to find the mother
to find the father
who do not own the house
who are not there.

Daphne

I was born of water,
my hair streaming back in waves,
my white robe whipping around me
like a sail.

How could I have loved Apollo?
It was my nature to flee
as it was his to pursue.
How can the deer love the hunter?

And if he had truly loved me,
he would never have wanted to pin me to the ground,
to fix me in his amber regard,
to paw me with his claws of stone.
If he had really loved me,
he would have let me go.

I felt his hot breath on my neck
rank as the maw of a ravenous dog.
So I called to my father the river,
thinking he'd sweep me to safety.
But my blood seemed to stop within me.
And as I felt my limbs stiffen,
I thought that Apollo had won.

I was to be his tree,
my boughs a sign of his triumph—
but only in the eyes of the world,
that medusa of false vision.

Underneath my bark
my sap still ran.
I abandoned my limbs to the wind.
The living water flowed into my roots
and up to my outermost branches.

I called to the creatures of river and wood,
and my words became tender new leaves.
Deer came to nibble them
and rabbits to sleep in their shade.
A small bird sang in my branches,
his song so high and clear it pierced my heart.

Los Angeles

There they were
all during my lonely childhood
in a small southern East Coast town—
shimmering softly
on some far horizon
like a host of lost angels.

Ah, but on our trips west
they'd gather, a bright band, around us,
and I knew I was really
a Japanese princess
come home to my true throne
in the high castle of their regard.

They were not ethereal creatures, though,
but solid and sure as rivers and mountains:

> Auntie Mamie, a buyer for a big department store,
> intuitively knew of your need
> for four pairs of pajamas.
> She could outfit you completely
> with accessories to match
> in thirty minutes flat.
>
> Auntie Ina hovered and fussed,
> patted and nagged
> (you could almost hear the nervous whirr
> of her wings),
> her sushi much more beautiful
> than most works of modern art.

Auntie Dora slips from room to room
serving five-course meals from her tiny kitchen.
She is small and lovely
as a Japanese doll,
her life as serene as a tea ceremony.

Auntie Gogo, true to her name,
always just back from an African safari,
a tour of Japan,
an Alaskan expedition.
She taught English
and brooked no nonsense.

Auntie Arlie glows softly
and roundly like a Buddha,
devoted to her Down syndrome son,
her one great calling to be beloved by all.

Auntie Mary, the church mouse,
always the last to be noticed,
still, though legally blind,
sends my children presents
she makes by hand for Christmas.

Auntie Lillie inclines her head
and flowers arrange themselves,
bread dough rises to attention.
The eldest, she is as poised
as a lotus on a long cool stem.
And down her spine there runs
a fine thread of Samurai steel.

And so this constellation of sisters
shone bright in the wide night skies
of my childhood.
Cast adrift far east of California,
I used them to find my way
as a sailor uses the stars.

My aunts are growing older.
One by one they fade
like stars as morning approaches.
But I know that on some farther shore
they'll be waiting
to show me how to come home.

Dismembered

For Colin and Kimi

Some acts of violence leave no corpse
just an invisible body ripped
arm and leg and head from torso,
spreading its clear blood across the sky.

Thus the end of our family—
each child flung to some far horizon:

Martin to a New England prep school.
I see him sitting in a bare schoolroom
winter light slanting
down through high windows,
his pencil clutched in a grubby hand,
cramped with effort and cold.

Out of place
among the sons of the northern elite,
he never made any close friends.
"Sylvie," he said again and again,
"I'm so alone. I'm so alone."

Anna to the coast of California.
I see her running through a high green meadow,
dotted with red flowers,
her hair whipping long and black behind her.
(Just out of sight
the meadow drops abruptly
to the rocks of the Pacific.)

After being bounced
back and forth across the country
for summer and Christmas vacations,

she developed a fear of flying.
They had to fill her with Valium
before putting her on the plane.

No Valium for me as I stood there waving
goodbye,
my inner ear hearing the muscles tear,
the flesh rip from bone.

Minus my family members,
I haunted the halls and stairwells
of my boarding school dormitory,
completely unconvinced of my existence.

We never returned to each other.
There was no place to return.

I've tried to piece together
a nest of broken twigs.
Occasionally I slip up
and call my son and daughter
by my brother's and sister's names.
And sometimes after a day of rain
when I'm driving home at sunset,
the clouds just starting to clear,
I look up to find the sky
filled with shreds of wings.
There I know in the high silver light
the angels are still screaming.

Beach Reunion

They come from all directions—
Boston, Denver, Oakland, Chapel Hill
Inevitably there's the fuss as each family arrives,
the luggage, the hugs, the warm words of love and welcome.

All of this begs the question, of course,
of how we got to be so far flung
that this is the only week of the year
we get to see each other.

Then we divide into groups—
the game players, the runners,
the readers, the nappers,
the young ones constantly clamoring
for their time at the beach.

Still here are the peace and jollity
that E. B. White wrote about,
the cheerful clamor that can only come
from a gathering of people who love each other.

I am the last one to leave the house,
and I stand looking out at the waves
rolling onto the sand,
going out, coming in,
pausing for no one,
moved only
by the shift of the tides.

Leaving Chapel Hill

I go out from this green womb
where the sun sifts down
through layers of leaves—
maple, dogwood, and oak.
These trees have rocked me and reared me.
In winter you can see they are rooted
in the sky, their branches reaching higher
than the noblest human thought.

In the beginning
a barefoot girl in a thin nightgown
stepped onto the soft wet lawn.
The myriad leaves of dogwood, camellia,
redbud and azalea
called my name in their many tongues.
Misty wisteria blurred the days into nights,
and honeysuckle wove spells
that turned fat toads
on plush grass
to princes on velvet pillows.

In the beginning was Morgan Creek,
long and brown as its name.
I crouched for hours on its bank,
a little maple and a mossy rock
nearby for company,
my playthings frogs and tadpoles,
crayfish and salamanders.

I took these sacred creatures back to the house
where I tried to recreate for them
the perfect life of the woods.

But they died in the still, dead water
of the aquarium, among the rotting leaves.
They must have needed the holy touch of the stream
to keep them alive.

My father still lives in a house
overlooking Morgan Creek.
I bring my children back to visit.
The walls resound with my son's hard rock,
and my daughter's laughter threads the rooms
like a little silver stream.

Sitting on a rock by the creek,
I gaze upstream.
I imagine that if I look hard enough
I can recapture the moment
before my exile.

And as I watch the water
playing over the rocks,
I become the barefoot girl
stepping onto the wet grass.
I hold out my arms
and the river rushes toward me,
like a mother, like a child.

“Just a Song at Twilight”

For Daddy

Do you remember
those long trips in the car
when I sat next to you for hours
and you taught me
every song you knew—
“Tell Me Why,” “Sailing Home,”
“Just a Song at Twilight”?

The light faded from the sky
and the darkness held us
in a world
that only a father and daughter
can make together.

Though the rough years came later,
and I didn’t see that much of you
after I turned fifteen,
still you taught me to sing.
And I still remember every word
of every song you taught me.

So though for many years
you’ve been gone,
in me your songs live on.

Blue Ridge Mountain Home

For my father

Three stone steps—
all that's left of the old cabin,
two large oaks—
now the only walls,
goldenrod and jewelweed growing
on ground where there used to be floor.

When I close my eyes I can
hear children laughing
smell bacon frying
in the wet morning air.

Hidden by the hemlocks,
a small stream flows beside me
down the mountain to the river—
cold and clear—
without regret.

What Is Left

I am one who follows the first-born of the dead.
I call his name—he will not answer.
I call his many names.
He walks, receding quickly, and will not turn his head.
He blends with the leaves of the trees and is gone
like a fish into shadowy water.

I have pried behind the blind eye
for the blind man has all of darkness
as the deaf-mute does all of silence
and only the handless man may reach God.

What is left after the world has broken
the pieces like bright glass jangling
in the cold eye of the sun?
What is left after the leaves have fallen,
their colors already fading
out of mind?
(The wind is shuffling through them
like a survivor through old papers
anxiously seeking a message or a sign.)

What is it that waits between our words,
breathes between our breaths?
Who waits just outside of the light of our lamps
like silence
to speak?

I bring you offerings of food.
See how meekly the carrot
lies on the plate.
And you will cut the meat.
You will chop the wood.
The sticks will crack
in your supple, long-fingered hands.

How gently you lay the logs on the grate
to make a cradle of flame.
And after you've lain in the place
that was hewn for you before time,
after the bed is split and I lie broken,
whose body is left
to hold the world together?

Now it is winter when things
draw back into themselves.
I wait in all the spaces between.
You could almost be he.
I look for your face in crowds
where I know you can't be.
Wherever I look it is you
who are missing.

Him I cannot see because
he is everywhere I look.
He is not only the rock
but where the rock is split.
He is the blind wound waiting,
the mute mouth calling.
I am absorbed into him like light.

I have seen behind the blind eye
a planet made almost new—
a naked girlchild running
through green transparent as fire.

She is calling my name.
She is calling my many names.
I reach for her with my handless arms.
She is coming, always, closer.
Now she is almost here.

II.
The One Who Is Leaving

Poem

What is this flimsy house of words?
porous as air, unstable as water.
You can't smell it, touch it,
or even eat it.
So what use is it anyway?

But the Buddhists claim
that what we think substantial
is really just an illusion,
evanescent as clouds,
ever-changing images
that leave not even traces
on an empty screen.

So unlike the slice of plump turkey,
the sweet, red dab of cranberry sauce,
the strains of the song I shared
with my love when he was alive,
my house of words doesn't lie.

It tells the truth by being
as flimsy as reality.

So come live with me in my house of words.
Who needs walls or windows or doors?
They're all just maya, anyway.

A Commuter in Wisconsin

Blue is the color of distance.
—Tennessee Williams, *Camino Real*

Here the land is loud.
Like a litany the lakes
repeat the refrain of sky.
The wind strums the grasses
and the corn speaks in tongues.

Honeysuckle embalmed
the place from where we'd come.
There anything could hide beyond a hill.
Here the land is almost flat:
there's no use denying a thing.

The roads after their crossings
stretch like arms
bared to the sky.
Oh, Lord, we have traveled
in the asphalt of your wounds.

In August when we came
pale blue flowers grew all along the roadside
(but no one seemed to know their name).
They squinted up at the glare of sky
like pious, near-sighted young men.

Quickly the land goes stark
like a charcoal drawing
until sunset when a bruise of color
spreads across the horizon.

The corn mutters dryly to itself
the road stretching like a tongue to water.
Raw the earth, with fields
plowed into its sides,
screams up black at the sky
until the snow responds with its mute white answer.

And now the green awakening—
the burst of wide-eyed rose
and shy anemone unfolding along the roadside,
again the grasses billowing their hymn.

Your arms like roads reaching toward me
shimmer with a promise of distance.
I am the one who is leaving
and the one who is coming home.

The Real Thing

I was miserable in those days
but rather beautiful—
straight dark hair to my waist
big brown eyes with a slight exotic tilt
slim as a wood nymph
all sunlight and shadow.

Then, though,
the whole world seemed negotiable—
more or less.

An actress off and on
I played the Young Lady
in Strindberg's *Ghost Sonata,*
slowly dying
in a pool
of lavender light.
I thought the world
a stage,
my life a perpetual dress rehearsal
for the real performance to come.

The world as it was
did not meet my specifications,
but I assumed that elsewhere
on some other plane
life was proceeding just as it should:
I had a lovely cookie-baking mother,
a father who took me on special trips to D.C.
and to the sweetheart banquet.

No wonder that as I walked
down my dormitory hall,
my footsteps sounded so hollow,
so unreal.

Was it when I first went into labor—
a huge fist shaking my body
as if it were a ragdoll,
bolts of lightning charging
up and down my spine—
that I understood
this was no dress rehearsal?

When they laid my son Aaron in my arms—
his mouth a small black hole
searching for my breast,
his dark, enormous eyes
devouring my face—

I must have understood
there was no other,
ideal form of Aaron.
Yes, it must have been at this moment
I knew I was playing for keeps.

Second Summer

The doctor reached into dripping dark
and plucked out a handful of light.

Son, you burn through my days—
the glittering minutes fly like sparks.
As you run through the house, the light
scatters like confetti.

At night by your bed
I switch on the lamp.
Golden, your hair curls
richly about your head.
I become lost in its intricacies
and do not want to be found.

At the store I cup in my hand a plum
and think of your head—how perfectly round,
of your apple cheek pressed fresh and firm
next to mine.

In our small house the sunlight is humming
the quiet hymn of your sleep.
Wind of a late afternoon
blows from across the fields,
moving over the pond,
lightly touching the willow fronds as it passes.

Heavy with its own weight
your head drops
for an instant on my lap.

Here is no simple light,
but instead the darkness of seeds:
the star at the apple's core.

Autumn has come round again,
and your hair is turning to brown with the leaves.
Yet even now at the touch of the windfall light
its strands glow golden once more.
Thus does the sun pluck its own.

Marriage

Always the first one up
to brew the coffee
you make the darkness clear.
As you call to me your voice
is sunlight through shadowy water.

You are my blue heron husband.
With my water body I lap at your legs.
My wind fingers touch the feathers
about your bony head.

Already with your waking movements
you've woven a white net of morning
to scoop me safe from sleep.

From the musk melon vines you grew in summer,
the shivering line of geese in flight,
the bright bits of Christmas ribbon, pine needles, and twine,
we have woven a garment of seams
that between us we will wear lightly
all the rest of our lives.

Closely we wrap round ourselves
the green hills of Wisconsin.
And at night we smolder softly,
folding into each other
as in wings.

For a Young Son in Autumn

In a reverie we drifted
through your first autumn
like leaves down the river
that runs through our picture book town:

The park—
its prim white bandshell,
birches and maples
arching to take us in.
The river floating through clouds
of dreamy willows
where goldfinches flit
like chips of errant sunlight.

The town cemetery
where we visit the gentle dead,
as slowly we walk through their slow autumn dream,
while among the spruce and pine
the blue jays split the air
with their prophetic cries.

The road
that leads up the hill
between two churches,
at the top the rows of houses
ending abruptly—
woods on one side,
cornfields on the other.
We turn around and the town
spreads out below us—
toy houses, factories, and stores—
all, my son, for you.

It was fall and we were rich.
The trees with infinite grace
gave up their leaves
and we wallowed in their wealth.

Already for me these images tend
to run together like watercolors,
and for you they'll be like dreams forgotten on waking.
But I want to keep the pages
of this your first picture book
crisp as autumn leaves,
their colors as sharp as your laughter
in the chill and crystalline air.

Beginnings

Do you remember when the world was new
as your first box of 64 crayons—
the promise of their waxy smell,
their perfect points,
their names like burnt sienna,
yellow ochre, jungle green, sky blue,
and carnation pink?

I did as I drove my son back to college
on a mid-October morning
along the wooded avenues of his campus,
the leaves in Crayola colors
swirling down around us,
their smell sharp in our nostrils.

Do you remember how quickly
the crayons lost their points
so you had to peel away the paper
until only blunt little nubs were left?

I did as I drove back from my son's college,
the afternoon light already foreshadowing darkness,
it's slant sharp as a scythe.

And I remembered another October
when I wheeled my son's stroller through piles
of fallen leaves
burnt golden as his hair.

When I got home,
I rushed up to my daughter's bedroom
and took a cigar box of crayons
out of her top desk drawer.

I fingered their papered sides
and held piles of them in my hands
as if they were pieces of gold.

Deeply I breathed in
the promise of their waxy smell—
their colors brilliant as leaves
on a mid-October morning.

Pale Son Gone

Even when you lived here,
you were always a little remote.

Sometimes I go and sit
in your pale blue room—
the air always cool, like you,
the white spires of Neuschwanstein Castle
rising in front of an icy lake
among snow-covered mountains
in the poster on your wall.

Always you seemed to elude me—
the fantasy novels I never quite got,
your perfect German I couldn't match,
the intricate pieces you composed on your guitar
but rarely performed for us.

So now you've moved to D.C.
And what is to keep you
from going on to Chicago,
to Seattle, Tokyo, Calcutta—
and finally to a place so remote
that no one can reach you?

This must be my fault, of course.
As mothers sometimes do with sons,
I let you go too early too far.
And now with twilight deepening to dusk
it's too late to call you in
to come home.

Now

The people pass—their voices rise and fall.
Sarah wakes not feeling well today.
The world goes by in shadows on her wall.

She covers her head with her afghan and curls up small.
Light shines through in red and blue and gold.
The people pass—their voices rise and fall.

The door slams shut—she hears her father call.
Sun bright, wind high—tree branches toss and sway.
The world goes by in shadows on her wall.

The telephone rings shrilly down the hall.
She lies beneath her afghan warm and still.
The people pass—their voices rise and fall.

Like sun and water, Sarah's thoughts are all
she needs to make bright flowers bloom and twine.
The world goes by in shadows on her wall.

With her stillness, softly she enthralls
the moment like a fawn in sunlit glade.
The people pass—their voices rise and fall.
The world goes by in shadows on her wall.

The World According to Sarah Grace

When the whole world goes gray
and I find myself waiting
in flat expanses
for some sign of life,
I take out Sarah's art.

"Come on," says the Voice of Doubt.
"Nothing was ever really this simple."
"But I have proof," I say,
as I display Sarah's drawings,
a world where things happen
in primary colors.

Here in bright red marker
is a picture of me, the Mom.
I stand in a circle of hearts
smiling and holding out my arms.
Behind me the daughter
stands in a smaller circle
joined with the first to make a figure eight—
"Me," says Sarah Grace.

And here are two people
sitting at a table—
a girl in pigtails and a print dress,
a man in a striped shirt and hat,
from which a blue flower grows.
Between them on the table
are good things to eat—
pink drinks with red straws
and bright food on white plates.

Here is a wedding party—
ladies in multicolored dresses,
a man with a smile that takes up his whole face—
all crowded together under some sort of arbor.
Any moment, now, you can tell
the most wonderful thing in the world
will happen.

Finally, here is my favorite:
a girl with piles of fruit at her sides—
purple circles of grapes,
yellow curves of bananas,
green and pink wedges of watermelon,
dotted with black seeds.
Above her head floats a fantasy of desserts—
chocolate bars and lifesavers in all colors,
popcorn and pink ice cream with a cherry.

In Sarah's world, you see,
everyone is always surrounded by good things,
and no one ever has to be alone.

"So what?" says the Voice of Doubt.
"So," I say, "I come from a world of blank spaces,
where things happen in shades of gray.
Sarah comes from me,
and these pictures come from Sarah.
This is magic enough for me."

They Got It Wrong in Genesis

For Aaron

What really happened is this:
In the beginning, Adam and Eve had fur
as soft and thick as a rabbit's.
But then they disobeyed and ate the apple,
using their new toy—
the knowledge of good and evil—
to classify and divide their world without end,
and placing, in the larger scheme of things
humans at the top, animals near the bottom.

Catching them at their game,
God stripped them of their fur,
leaving them pink and naked as newborn rats.
"So you think you're that much better
than my furred and feathered creatures?" God said.
"Then go and dwell in a separate place."
And ever since then, we've lived in the exile
of houses.

The problem with houses is
most of them are too dark inside,
and except for us, some germs and dust mites
(and maybe a stray ant or cockroach),
everything in them is dead.
No wonder, then, that we're such a morbid race.

And now when we go outdoors,
nature exacts its revenge
for the arrogance of our forebears:

cold chills or sun burns,
bees sting, mosquitoes bite,
and we retreat indoors where it's safe and deadly.

But on a day like this one in early fall,
when the rabbits hop to the front of their hutch to be petted
and sunlight touches your hair with grace;
when you can bury your face in a cushion of yellow
chrysanthemum blossoms,
each one pressing against your skin like a kiss—

On a day like this,
God suffers us
not to be separated
but welcomes us back—
if just for this moment—
into the land of the living.

For Shelly

In celebration of *The Andrew Poems*[1]

When it was time to go,
you filled my arms with white roses—
so many I had to cradle them
as if I held a child.

These weren't your haughty court lady kind
but open-faced dairymaid roses,
spilling in cheerful confusion
over the low stone wall—
their scent not heavy
but fresh as morning rain.

I had come to help prepare your poems,
to deliver them soft and round and whole
into a world of sharp angles and hard edges.

Eyes blurred from too much revision—
the words as meaningless
as birds' feet tracks in sand—
we stepped onto the lawn that slopes to the river,
and the world split suddenly open into water and sky.

The river glowed serenely
with the soft light of early evening,
the roses tumbling over the wall
like happy, unruly children
on their way down the lawn to the river.

---

[1] *The subject of all the poems in this book is Shelly's son Andrew, who at five years old had drowned in the river near Shelly's house.*

I buried my nose in their blossoms
as I sometimes do in my daughter's hair:
Now, I thought, *I know why I'm here.*

After I'd brought them home
and put them in a vase,
my five-year-old daughter asked,
"Are the roses still alive?"
I just didn't know
how to answer.

Sleepover

Ten o'clock
and the sun already spilling
through my daughter's windows
pooling in the folds of her comforter
(the one she chose herself from a catalog—
ivory slashed with red Chinese characters).

Beneath the covers,
Sarah and her friend are curled together
warm and golden as lion cubs,
Sarah's fine dark hair swirling
into her friend's thick, honey-blonde curls.

They will not emerge for another two hours,
but in my mind's eye I watch them
from the sad height of my years.
Below they laugh and dance
at thc cdgc of thc sca,
sand warm beneath their feet.
The seafoam seems to them
lacy as their lingerie.
the glittering water brilliant
as the gems in the cheap jewelry
they're constantly giving each other.

They can't see what I see—
how the sun flashes
off each little wave
like a knife-blade.

But it's no use calling
to them. I am too far.
And even if they heard me,
they'd only giggle and wave
before plunging into the water.

Leavings

My daughter loves all things red—
          strawberries, raspberries, cherries,
          nail polish, lipstick, rubies, and hearts.

So how, after all the stores we've haunted,
catalogs pored over together,
can she bear to leave the room
she so carefully decorated
with its red-flowered rug,
cranberry blinds,
and plum-colored pillows?

Easily enough, it seems,
since these days,
she's always eager to be somewhere else:
Starbucks, the movies, or the beach
with friends.

She's begun to shed
her childhood things
as casually as on prom night
she shrugged off
the blood-red dress
we'd bought her at some expense
and left it in a pool
on her bedroom floor.

In a few weeks
she'll be off to college.

On the kitchen table
the tops of the strawberries
she ate
before going out for pizza
with friends
lie festive as
little green windmills
after the county fair.

Easter Weekend

We drive such a long way,
after missing her so much,
to give our college daughter her Easter basket
with chocolate bunny, yellow Peeps,
and malted pastel eggs—
the usual phony symbols of fecundity.
Perhaps a fool's errand
for a few quick hugs
and a couple of meals and walks
before she breezes back to her boyfriend
and her real life at college.

But as always there are the unexpected gifts—
the mountains rising like gracious hosts
to greet us,
the blush of barely budding leaves
on the hillside.
And even after the many rapes of the year—
Israel and Gaza
Ukraine and Sudan—
still the dogwoods float
white and virginal
among clouds of flowering Judas blooming
from thousands of tiny purple wounds
in their sides.

Redundant Abundance

I love that my daughter
is fearlessly redundant.
At the end of each email,
after saying,
"I love you lots and lots and lots,"
she writes, "Love, Sarah."

There's a lot to be said for repetition.
The little late-season daffodils all turn
identical faces to the sun,
their orange centers
like identical kisses.

Only humans aim for the "unique"
all trying to be more unique than others.
On the other hand,
a daffodil never tries
to be anything but itself.

As for my daughter's
insistent, vociferous, and repetitious love,
I gladly accept the sudden hugs,
the multiple hearts
bespeckling each text,
the passionate "I love you's"
at the end of every phone call.

Because sometimes too much
of a very good thing
is just the right amount.

Early Spring Moment

For Sarah Grace

Bent with the weight of winter
the crab-apple tree spreads over our front yard,
branches impossibly twisted
as if in long and convoluted thought.

But on this first warm morning
fog catches on stiff gray limbs
growing clusters of tiny leaves.

Somewhere an old man
puts down his newspaper,
looks out the window,
and thinks for a moment
of his granddaughter.

Spring Song

Sing a song of beginnings
quick bliss of crocuses
opening purple lips to chill air,
tendrils of clematis twining
lithe stems around weathered trellises,
yellow forsythia exploding into stars.

I am no longer young
but still the spring wind
slips through the slats
of the old wooden fence,
and my heart bursts into blossom.

Ode to Sixteen-Bean Soup

Glory be to the black-eyed pea,
coy, petite with your discreet white spot,
to the kidney bean, red organ of the earth,
to the navy bean in your spotless whites,
to the cranberry bean with your avant-garde streaks,
to the great northern, baby lima, black turtle,
pinto, lentil, barley, and green pea.

Glory be to all the beans,
sparkling in the colander, gems of the earth,
smelling like fresh, wet grass in the morning,
then bubbling in the pot,
sprinkled with cumin, red pepper, and thyme,
blending with ham and stewed tomatoes,
and finally held in my mouth,
rich steam rising to my nostrils,
slipping down my throat to become
flesh of my flesh, bone of my bone.
Hallelujah. Amen.

The Summer Kingdom

So it all comes down to this:
A two-story brick house
with garage and large deck
on a half-acre lot in the suburbs.

I was raised in a forest Eden,
my earliest memories red camellias
floating in crystal bowls,
dogwood white in a sea
of redbud and new green.

Even now in my native town
my father lives in a house of wood
designed to fade to the silver
of the surrounding trees,
built on a hill overlooking a stream
where masses of pink rhododendron
blossom every April.

Still, I'm not surprised to find myself here,
having long accepted exile
as my natural condition.

But I can't help chafing
at the state of my neighbors' yards:
the one bare except for a lawn,
by now mostly weeds,
that my neighbor occasionally mows
to resemble the head of an ugly kid
with a buzz cut;

the other bare even of lawn,
since, for want of something better to do
the two dogs there have completely dug it up—
a mudhole in rain,
a cracked desert in drier weather.

By comparison our place doesn't look so bad—
the house flanked by two tall magnolias,
large willow oaks in front and back,
a cedar, a dogwood, some pines.

When we first moved here in the fall
we planted bulbs and a few more trees—
a maple, an apple, a weeping cherry.
It took an act of faith to put them—
then no more than sticks—into the ground.
But, lo, in spring their leaves popped out
and the flower bulbs bloomed in waves of color—
daffodils, hyacinths, irises, and lilies.

Now in summer
the gracious magnolia
lifts up huge blossoms
as cool and lemony
as a mother's hand
on a sweaty little forehead.
The mourning doves coo
long blue corridors
through the white-hot days,
and cicadas build high
round towers of sound
to create a summer kingdom.

Now at forty-two,
the first time in my vagabond life,
I dare to plant something in the ground,
and count on being around
to see it come up in the spring.

It all comes down to this:
earth's body,
broken for us
into half-acre lots
in the suburbs—
these our only
gardens

Late Afternoon in Early Spring

Is it possible to live without feasting on death?
—Walker Percy, *Love in the Ruins*

It's one of those days when the air's so light and warm
your body feels like dandelion fluff,
a day when there's no point in doing a thing—
for what could match the forsythia's grace,
the pink camellia's perfection, the generosity
of white crab apple blossoms?
And so I'm content to lie in my hammock
breathing in the smell of new-mown grass.

My Japanese neighbor hangs her wash on the line.
Lovely and slim, black hair to her waist,
she slips between the clothes and sheets
like a sliver of moon through clouds.
She spends her time studying English,
as she waits for her navy husband's return.
But her English never seems to improve,
and she misses her family in Japan.

The two little Indian girls from next door
speaking in soft English accents
wander through the overgrown grass of their yard
in long red and blue print dresses.

(Their mother, plump and smelling of cooking,
stays inside and tries to hide
from America, but what she sees on her telly
only confirms that dangers lurk
around every corner, behind every bush.)

Our other next-door neighbor works for the power company.
Here he is, large and white, on his red riding mower
his body overflowing the small seat.
When he's not mowing his lawn,
he spends his time trying to revive
the VCR, weed eater, toaster oven—
one dead machine or another—
his wife at a mall or garage sale
shopping for the one last item
that will make their lives complete.

Their two small children, a boy and girl,
are often left to themselves.
When they're not watching TV
they trail around their backyard
clutching Barbies and Power Rangers,
their pale faces wet with mucus and tears,
wailing like little lost spirits.

I used to try to get all my neighbors together
for potluck suppers or cookouts,
but someone was always busy—
my Japanese neighbor waiting for a phone call,
my Indian ones for a relative's visit,
my American ones for the plumber.

So I turned to my yard instead,
planting every inch with bushes and flowers.

But when I dug too deep, I uncovered
a network of thick white roots,
their surfaces stained with red,
their source a mystery.

It's getting late, but I hate to go in—
such afternoons are so rare.
Against the chain-link fence
the pyracantha stretches
thorny, twisted branches,
and the columbine close by
drips endless red and white blossoms.
The last rays of sunlight linger—
touching the crab apple's trunk,
the chain-link fence, the camellia petals,
the lawnmower seat, the blades of new grass—
like the fingers
of a dying
savior.

A Woman Lovely

As I stand with my cart full of groceries—
ground beef, yogurt, apples, and toilet tissue—
I must look to the checkout lady
and the other customers
like any middle-aged woman—
my hair threaded with silver,
the flesh under my chin starting to sag,
my stomach, hips, and legs,
expanding in all directions.

They don't understand that this
is not how I look at all:
Inside this middle-aged body,
my eyes glow large and dark
as Anna Karenina's;
my glossy black hair
feathers my lovely face—
neck and waist imperially slim,
elegant legs as long
as a thoroughbred filly's.

When I was younger
I was almost beautiful—
slim with long brown hair to my waist,
but underneath my golden skin
I was rather miserable,
huddled up like a child in the cold.

In those days, I wore my body
as the rhinoceros in Kipling's story
must have worn his breadcrumb-filled skin.
No wonder I was a little edgy.

After I’ve loaded my groceries into the car,
I slip into the driver’s seat.
Reveling in my secret loveliness,
I settle into my loosened body
as in a capacious armchair
after a long but rewarding day.

After Eight Years of Suburban Living

The cookie jar wasn't always full
or the neighbors especially friendly.
My daughter's room was usually a mess
and sometimes my son's heavy metal
sounded as if it might saw the house in two.

But late one summer afternoon
as I stood at the second-story window
the green of grass and willow and pine
deepening to dusk,
a dozen fireflies lit up at once—
as if someone had tossed a handful of stars
onto the darkening lawn.

Blueberries

For Eleanor

We had to fight the birds for them,
surrounding the bushes with nets
so that we could only pick them
one at a time
reaching thumb and forefinger
through the mesh
like the beak of a bird.

The berries felt
round and soft and firm
as nipples,
worth the blood
the mosquitoes sucked
from our arms and legs
as we picked.

And in spite of the four
tablespoons of cornstarch,
when I cut the pie
I'd made with the berries,
the purple filling rose
and stained the white flesh of the crust,
flowing onto the dessert plate
smelling of earth and sunlight
tasting so sharp and sweet
it sliced my tongue into song.

The Inner Room

For Jeffrey, Aaron, and Sarah

Undoing Christmas, we wrap
the green ball, the red bird, the gold bell
in layers of tissue paper like drifts of snow.
This January night as cold
as black water under white ice.
I hear the wind sneaking under the door and know
someday one of us will go out
and not come back.

But we've built a fire on the hearth,
where it blazes like a roaring lion
devouring the night.
I've watched it hollow a log
to make an inner room
lined with glowing feathers of orange and gold.
Here, I think, we could all live forever,
if we could sing together with tongues of flame,
each life an alleluia in one song.

III.
Will the Circle Be Unbroken?

To a Poet

Look here:
I read poetry because
I'm drowning.
So, please, spare me your flimsy words:
idle reflections,
whimsical images,
subtle cerebrations.
Throw me instead a line
muscular and tough as a tropical vine,
and hand over hand,
word over word,
haul me safe to shore.

Crow Caucus

In the twittering dawn of early spring,
a crow's caw cuts across my sleep,
a jagged scissor of sound.
Later they gather in the tall backyard pines,
a raucous cacophony of crows.
They argue back and forth about some important matter
(maybe it's my husband's cancer):

"Of course," one caws.
"Unh-unh," says another.
This jury of black-suited birds
seems unable to reach a verdict.
"Could be," caws one.
"Couldn't," says another.
I think they must still be deadlocked
because
even now we don't know the answer.

The Wisdom of Trees

Though their leaves are still green,
the trees know that winter is coming.
The branches of the dogwood
nod their leafy heads together
like a group
of conspiring old men.

"Yes, now the air is still warm,
but the cold creeps up our trunk
and reaches our leaves.
Soon, very soon
the great change will come
and it will be time for us
to leave.
This is the way of all things
green and golden."

So say the trees,
and we know in the cold of our bones,
it is true.

Sunburst

To Andrew York

It's a miracle
that you could take the sun
and compress it into
so few guitar notes.

As I listen it's almost
as if I wake early
on a Saturday morning
to a bowl of oranges
in a bright yellow bowl
before strolling down
a sunny street in Aix-en-Provence.

At the end
you shatter the sun
into trillions of scintillating bits
that brighten for a moment
my steadily darkening world.

Endless Winter

I had always dreaded
the dark of winter,
the days cut brutally short,
the afternoon shadows lengthening,
reaching out like the ghosts
of my childhood nightmares.

But I did love
the Christmas season
that began with your birthday
in early December.
This one, though, was marred
by a nagging worry about
the numbness in your right foot
that worsened until you could hardly walk.

In early February,
my month of many deaths,
we got the diagnosis:
"glioblastoma multiforme,"
I read on the radiologist's report.
And even before the doctor appeared
to let us know,
funereally solemn,
what this meant,
I could tell by its name
that this disease would
blast our dreams
and with great glee
mutilate our lives for good.

I knew it to be a shape shifter
a many-headed Hydra
that would grow new limbs
faster than they could be severed.

I sat by your hospital bed
with the snow falling endlessly
outside your window.
And my only wish was that
we could stay this way forever,
that time would freeze in place
and winter would never end.

Fast forward a year
to the next February
when the symptoms
suddenly returned,
and I knew beyond a doubt
that this was it.

When I held you,
I could feel a tremor
deep in your body
that told me it was shutting down
like a worn-out engine.
This winter like the last one
was unusually harsh.
The snow weighed us down
like the row of twisted junipers
that we had to have removed.

You lasted through late spring,
the end of my sixtieth year.
With temperatures in the nineties,
the whole world seemed to wilt
at once. And I would have given anything
to turn the clock back to winter,
the endlessly falling snow
somehow suggesting
we would have so much time left
together.

Now I no longer dread the dark of winter
because after you died, it seemed the norm.
There were no other seasons.
Winter was just the way it was
for good.

The Angel's Dream

For Jeffrey

I woke under a harsh and alien sun.
Red and orange flowers blared and bled
into my eyes.
"Those are just azaleas,"
someone said.

I kept asking people again and again,
"How can I get home?"
But they looked at me oddly
and shook their heads.
"We don't know where your home is.
That is something only you can know."
they said.

But the ground was gray
and hard and rough
and hurt my feet so much
I could not take a step.

So I screamed a high and silver scream
as only an angel can scream.
I called to you by every name I knew.
I screamed so loud I split the sky in two
("That's just a streak of lightning,
someone said.")

And as the sky opened,
I woke up in your arms
of feathery white clouds.

“Oh my love, my precious love,”
I said,
“for a terrible moment I thought
you had forsaken me.”

“I left you, yes,” you said,
“but you have not been forsaken.”

Fish and Cars

As I drive on my way to the pool,
listening to Schubert's trout quintet,
I imagine our cars are fish,
swimming down the river of road,
but then we so plainly are not.
At a red light we stop, at a green we go
not flowing like fish
but jerking clumsily through our lives.

Most cars are gray or tan,
not like the bright shoals
of tropical fish
in red and blue and gold

I like to think that after our deaths,
we will flow like schools of fish,
unobstructed by any physical thing
as translucent as the water
around us.

But I'm on my way to the swimming pool,
where I will swim like a fish in heaven.

Faith

In last summer's drought
the little fir
that grew near our front steps
died.
And so this spring
in the space it left,
I decided to plant coreopsis from seed.
I was drawn to the picture
of the intricate golden flowers on the packet—
perennials that would "bloom the first year."

After I'd dug up the soil
to make the bed,
I saw I'd made a raw black wound
in the earth.
So this is why no one else plants from seed—
why my neighbors fill their new beds
with ready-grown plants so quickly.

And now I can only wait.
Anxious for some sign of life
I check the round bed
that looks like a freshly dug grave
for a family pet.

When a few sprouts finally emerge,
they are hopelessly nondescript.
I can't even pull up the weeds—
I don't know which they are.
All I can do is go on
and water the weeds with the flowers.

Not here the explosion of golden blooms
that should have crowned my labors,
the stunning image that should have completed
this poem.

Only this raw black earth,
these tiny green leaves,
this long dark ache in the heart.

Jazz Trio

In the cold hard air of November
the concert hall fills with a warm sea of sound.
The bass player plumbs the depths of the water,
the swish of the drums like sunlight brushing waves,
the piano arpeggios a school of bright fish
darting into the coral.
The broad-shouldered bass player
pulls his bow over the strings—
the muscles of the music.
The sticks of the long-limbed drummer
seem to come from his bones.
The bird of a man perched at the piano
trills, and the blood
moves through the body
till it sways in its chains like the sea.

No Handel or Bach,
picky about beginnings, middles, and ends,
this music flows on like an everlasting stream,
like a carpet of stars unrolling
through the darkness.
Mercer, Brown, Porter, Corea—
It could go on forever.

This is music to dive in,
a big warm mama, who wraps you in her arms
and rocks you, chanting your name
over and over like the sea.

I came to this concert
from a cold, dry world,
my heart as shriveled
as a Japanese mushroom.
But now
it springs from its shell
like the paper flowers
we used to drop into water—
bursting into blossom.

Forest Path, Cezanne

After the dizzy heights   and plunging depths
there is after all   nothing left
but to go on   putting the inevitable foot
in front of the other,   nothing but the brown dirt
path and the trees   growing into deeper
blues   and greens
until   I am
invisible   even to
my   self.

Will the Circle Be Unbroken?

She moved in circles, and those circles moved.
—Theodore Roethke

Early morning and the schoolchildren's voices
begin as a trickle of sound, building until
their shouts and laughter rise like a flock of birds
suddenly flying.

Later, as I walk across campus
in the spring sunlight
a young man is blowing bubbles
as his long-skirted girlfriend swirls
a hula-hoop around her slender hips.

And then there was that other April morning
My daughter's voice on the phone
sounding slightly alarmed—
something about a shooting on campus—
but then the horror slowly growing
like a mouth opening wider and wider
in an endless silent scream:

"Mom, I don't know what's happening—
I keep hearing the sirens."

The news coming on the TV
in short bursts like machinegun fire:
two killed, eleven, twenty-five and counting.

The next day a picture of my daughter's friend,
smeared across the front page of the paper
being carried like a side of meat

out of the classroom building;
at night the students standing
in a circle of candle lights;
the missing faces in the dining hall,
the dormitories and classrooms.

Will the circle be unbroken?

Meanwhile the flowers piling up—
dogwoods, redbuds, camellias, azaleas—
in waves of white and purple and red.
No one had ever seen
a more heartbreakingly beautiful April.
And now the seasons have spun round
three times more.
My daughter graduated from college last spring;
she works in a different city now,
and I am still waiting for someone
to unbreak the circle.

In the morning the children stream
toward the school across from my house,
their sweaters, skirts, pants, and backpacks
a kaleidoscope of color.

I was one of these children
I was the long-skirted college girl
I was one of her teachers.

And for a moment I see myself as
a very old woman turning around,
arms opening wide
to the child I once was
running toward me,
lips parted, eyes bright,
fine hair streaming backward
in the first light of spring.

And when at that final moment
I hold her close in my arms,
then will the circle be unbroken?

IV.
Early Fall

Four Years Later

Time, recently, weighs heavy on my heart—
as if the four years' worth of days
since you died
have silted up around my soul.
As I go my daily round,
I always think
how you would have loved this
or hated that.
Your words haunt my days.

But would I have it any other way?
For this is what is left—
stray phrases, shreds of memory,
a whiff of magnolia
from some long-ago spring
when you were here
and all was well.

But I have to beware
of memory's propensity
for editing out the bad,
saving only those better moments.
The lesser ones have all vanished
dark water under the bridge,
lost in the sludge of time
where, maybe, they belong.
The best ones have risen
from the sea
like shining stars against the dark night
that now I call my life.

In the Locker Room

There's a woman at the other end of the room
who keeps turning her head to look at me.
She reminds me vaguely of someone I once knew,
but I don't think this is her.

That other woman was lovely in her bones
lovely because beloved
by a tall, slim man with a dark chocolate voice,
whose students loved to eat his words,
who used to stride across campus in a tweed sports coat,
button-down shirt open at the throat,
bony, long-fingered hands, high forehead,
and a heart-breaking smile.

It was rumored that he adored his wife,
and the female students wondered
how she could be so special
as to be deserving of *him.*

But she knew he had sanctified her
with the sacrament of his touch,
crowned her with honor high
as a redwood tree on a hill—
that her words to him were the sighing
of small birds in early morning.

But, as I said, this woman can't be her.
This one is dumpy, face lined and weary.
You can tell she goes home to an empty house,
eats her Lean Cuisine in front of the TV, and crawls
gratefully into her cold, white bed by nine o'clock.

So you say that's a mirror at the other end of the room?
No, that just can't be. Though that woman may be a widow,
she can't possibly be me.

Friday the Thirteenth, March 2015

For Judy on her birthday

Winter clamped down hard
and we cowered under its weight.
The clusters of daphne buds
stayed clenched in tight fists
refusing to bloom in the iron-cold air.

But last night when I came home
their sweet scent filled the darkness with
the extravagant promises of spring.

Their tiny blooms had burst open
like pink mouths opening to breathe
for the very first time
opening to sing
even in the dark and cold
the impossible songs of spring.

Tsunami

For Allen

After the first disaster,
I took stock of the damage—
Broken husks that once had held
all the life I knew.

And after some hesitation
(since, unlike a dolphin, I couldn't
will myself to die),
I started to rebuild:
a firm foundation of sturdy brick,
walls of solid wood, a roof of tidy shingles.
Finally, after a few false starts
and years of strenuous labor,
I was satisfied:
My life was tight and neat and dry.

Until you
swept through
in deep blue waves
one after another,
so that soon there were dolphins
swimming through the bedroom,
sharks circling in the kitchen,
bright fish flitting up the stairwell—
and slowly the walls began to fall,
the foundation to wash away,
and all I had left was what you brought—
the ruins of love.

Afternoon Delight

Today I felt myself to be
perfectly hollow.
And you were many rivers
flowing through me
coming together
leaping over the rocks
and falling
down
down
down
to rest
into the cool, clear pools
below.

Moment

For Allen, as always

Your eyes are golden, leonine,
like deep water struck with sunlight.
My fingers trace the clean lines
of your face, flowing over your forehead,
and beneath them I sense the spinning
of fierce suns and wild, far-flung stars.

My fingers trickle down your neck
and join the long river of your torso
until they lap at shores,
dark and unexplored—
as those woods where
side by side
we beached our kayaks,
felt the light breeze on our faces,
watched the tiny fiddler crabs
dart into their holes,
and heard for a moment
that perfect silence
no human voice can break.

Surfer Dude

Another one for Allen

I'd always assumed, perhaps unfairly,
that most surfers were mentally deficient.
So it's probably only poetic justice
that I've become utterly smitten with one.

But in my mind's eye, I see you,
flecked with sand and sun,
a giant wave curling around you
so close it seems likely
to swallow you whole.

And I? I only wish
the wave were me.

The Language of Waves

I sit with my morning coffee
and watch the little waves
break near the shore.

And each one seems to murmur your name
over and over and over
in a chorus of voices singing
my love for you back to me.

Look—there's another one—
there and there and there.
But it's not enough
because I want you
here and here and here.

The Man Who Wasn't There

For Allen with love

There once was a man whom no one knew.
Could it be that he was you?
His eyes were brown as was his hair.
His looks, I'd say, were good to fair.
But when asked to describe him his family would swear
they were certain he just wasn't there.

And yet the women continued to stare
because he was so attractive
for someone who wasn't there.
They could make him whatever they wanted:
a golden idol on an altar of air,
but somehow they'd be disappointed
to find that he still wasn't there.

Meanwhile, the man whom no one knew
wondered what about him was real and true.
But his relatives had no time to spare,
and not even the women who continued to stare
could help him to find himself anywhere
because they knew that he just wasn't there.

Love's Labor Lost

To each person you love
you give a piece of yourself,
and you may never get it back.

In my mind I'm saying goodbye.
I see him off at the shore
in his kayak.
He's laughing and clowning
as always
that elastic face of his
scrunching up and stretching out
in the ways I find so endearing.

He waves cheerily as the boat
gets further and further from shore
until it's just a tiny speck
on the ocean's huge horizon.

And I wonder what happens
to the piece of myself I gave him
after he leaves.
Does he carry it like a stone
in his pocket,
not even knowing it's there?

Or maybe it's a handful of coins
scattered among his things.
And just when he thinks
he's out of luck and money
he finds a piece
to pay for his next meal.

Or it could be
a soft, cool hand
touching his hot forehead
as he lies sick in bed.

Maybe he sees it
in the sunset
above his beloved ocean,
pastels of pink, peach, and lavender
deepening to gashes
of purple, red, and gold.

Or hears it
in a few bars of the song
I sang him
on some magnolia-scented night.

What I do know
is that where my love once was
they'll be a hole
the size of his bony fist
in my chest.
And all I can do is pray
that I didn't give away
a piece of myself
for nothing.

Foof, the Covid Kitten

I know he's just
a fluff of dust in this vast universe,
but to me he's so much more.

He came into my life
on a cold, dark day
when I was hollowed out by sorrow,
weary of the sad little rituals of my days,
sickened by the thought
of the thousands dying
for want of a little care.

My life was a dry, brittle shell
until my little cat leapt in
as if into a flowery meadow.

I love his velvety ears, his amber eyes
alight with curiosity and mischief,
his black fur sleek as sealskin,
his prim white paws
that sneaked into my heart
until it was full to overflowing.

He can make a game of anything—
a random piece of ribbon,
an elusive dust bunny.
And oh his prodigious leaps
as he turns a half somersault in the air
in pursuit of his favorite toy!

And so he makes me laugh
in peals of sunlight.
Thus it is that joy can blossom
in the driest desert,
even the one in my heart.

Revelation

Subject to the leaden depression
that often overtakes me around aisle 3
of the grocery store,
I saw a youngish man
whose black hair stood out
in sharp spikes all over his head.
He wore a garish yellow T-shirt
on whose front was a square
filled with ugly pink cherry blossoms
overwritten by the word TOKYO.
He wore jeans
and high-top brown shoes.
He moved awkwardly
as if he wasn't quite sure he belonged
in the grocery store.

He gave me hope.
Here was a man
whose clothes betrayed his condition.
I appear in disguise
in appropriate capris
with a perky cotton top.
But this man's clothes showed
that in all honesty
he was a misfit like me.

Sophia

I remember her only as one spark
among many—
children running barefoot
through the San Francisco house.

"Oh the trees they do grow high,
and the leaves they do grow green."
She was our green leaf
who played among the branches
with the others.
This, though,
was never enough
to make her happy.
She wanted to go higher
than the highest tree could take her.

And so now she leaves us,
a pale, slender leaf,
slipping down a swift-running stream
to who knows where.

Early Fall

For Allen and Allison

As I walk back through the campus
after the poetry reading,
the soft air of early autumn
lifts a strand of hair from my temple
in a gesture more infinitely gentle
than any mother's touch.

Is this really the same world where
on a day very like this one,
a crazed man hauled trunk loads
of semi-automatics up 32 floors
just so that, a few hours later,
he could fire thickets of bullets
into the tender bodies
of the hundreds of men and women
dancing below?

It was, in fact, the dancing that saved her,
her left arm raised to catch the bullet
that would have slammed into her chest instead.

We picked out flowers to send to her—
hydrangeas, roses, and lilies
the color of morning sunlight.

Gently raised in the suburbs
of a southern East Coast town,
she was everybody's darling.
Here she is on her Facebook page,
sunlight streaming down golden hair
that in turn streams down golden shoulders.

And can this be the same hair
so clotted with dark blood
that even days after the shooting,
it couldn't be brushed?

Today her father arrived
at Sunrise Medical Center.
I can see his big-boned hand
on the white coverlet
of her hospital bed,
the hand that tied the kayaks
on the truck and guided
her bucking surfboard
into the waves.
There's something golden about him too—
the burnished tan, the tawny,
slightly leonine eyes.

He looks down,
and his gaze falls on her face
like a shaft of sudden sunlight.

Dinner for Six
(A Tragedy of Comic Proportions)

For Janet Peery

It was one of those nights—
The oysters wouldn't open,
the sauce wouldn't thicken,
and the phone rang just
as I was serving dinner.

The magician who could salvage this evening
would have thought it a breeze
to spin straw into gold
or to raise Lazarus from the dead.

As we were eating,
I couldn't help seeing
the black veins in the shrimp,
the brown edges on the camellia petals.

After we'd walked the guests to their cars,
I looked up to find the full moon's face
covered with dirty blotches.

Snow Day

In the dark of early morning,
I open a blind to find
the world unexpectedly turned white.

After breakfast,
I whirl around the kitchen
making Brunswick stew
and then go upstairs to meditate,
slightly tired but glad to have put
the stew on to simmer.

I look out the window to see
a purple finch at the feeder,
a cardinal pecking around below.
and the snow lying along the dark branches
of trees like a lover.

I sit, and the silence
settles around me like snow.
My hands are a lotus bud
waiting to open,
and I know beyond reason
that in just one deep breath,
I can hold the world.

V.
A Form of Limitation

Poetry as Found Art

A poem doesn't come as whole cloth.
Rather it's stitched together,
a patchwork of colors,
formed of little catkins
from the pine trees,
of scraps of paper
and bits of ribbon and grass,
rather as a bird makes a nest.

Frost has called a poem
"a momentary stay against confusion,"
but uncertainty too
must be woven onto its loom.
until we are quite certain
of how little we know.

Swimming Lesson

Every day at noon
two Japanese gentlemen come
to swim in the university pool.
Choosing adjacent lanes,
they breaststroke along together
serene as swans,
their chatter soothing as
the gentle splashing of water.

Then there are the rest of us:
counting minutes, laps, and calories,
arms slicing, feet pumping,
envisioning ourselves as slim, brisk, and fit
as each of us swims alone
through all that cold blue water.

To My Cancer

Who are you, and why are you here?
You appear in my dreams as faceless
furry creatures, who burrow, unwanted,
into my bed.

Are you here to fill the hollow
that was left when my husband died?
If so, I do not need you.
My life already brims full
of laughter and tears,
flowers and faces of children;
of trials and triumphs
and pesto and crème caramel.

It's true the hollow was there
right after he died,
and I dragged myself through the days,
and weeks and years, pretending
to all who asked that I was all right.
And this must have taken its toll.

But as nature abhors a vacuum,
grass and flowers grew
in that fallow soil,
and now I don't need
any extra growth within me.

So melt away
and blend into the flow of my blood
so your sibling cells
can do their good work.

I imagine you must have had some purpose,
but this isn't true anymore.
So please leave and let me live
my rich and unlikely life.

Hymn to the Chesapeake: A Response

For Bob

I have bathed in the waters of your words,
swum among the salty swells of the Chesapeake,
danced with ghosts of pirates and sailors,
scuttled with the shadows of crabs across the sand,
blown with the wind through a thousand white sails,
and sat on the porch with Old Kate Bull,
chewing the fat and the lean.

I've heard the cries of the black oyster hucksters,
tasted the salty crust on the *Priscilla's* keel,
seen the barges and tugs slip by me in the fog,
flipped and flashed with the fishes caught in your net,
felt the rough hand of Blackbeard on my shoulder,
and gone ashore with Johnny to collect my pay.

I've flown high with the osprey
over the bay's trembling waters,
ridden in the orange boat past so many green islands,
seen through the eye of the Cape Charles Lighthouse,
the prism that divides the colors and the days
and brings them together in one guiding light.

Popcorn

You had an inordinate love
of popcorn.
We would eat it while you watched
a football game on TV,
and I would sit beside you
not caring for a moment about the game
but wanting only to be near you
while we ate popcorn.

After we'd shared a bowl
you declared
you could have eaten the whole thing
by yourself.
It's one of my intense regrets
that we didn't simply make you
your own bowl of popcorn.

In the three years after your death
I couldn't eat a single kernel of popcorn,
but now it has been ten years
and today I made a bowl of popcorn
and in your honor,
I ate the whole thing.

In Memory of Ti

So many things he didn't have:
a car in the garage,
letters after his name,
bills, doubts, ambitions,
a job, a wife, a child—
all the trappings thought necessary
to make you somebody.

A few things he had
and loved
with all his simple heart:
his videotapes of old movies,
his Mickey Mouse tie and suspenders,
his season tickets to operas,
his father, his sisters,
his church, his God.

His body, wrong from birth,
ordained a life of pain:
endless drugs and needles,
procedures and operations.
His pale cheeks never grew hair.
His large head wobbled like a flower
too heavy for its stem,
eyes the clear high blue
of an early summer sky.

Without the usual clutter,
his life held plenty of space
for us.

He was always ready to listen,
to crack a joke about his condition,
to describe the T-shirt his sister
had given him for Christmas,
to assure us of the many blessings
of God.

Near the end
when he lay in his hospital bed,
his sister tried to pull a sheet over his legs
all mottled from needles and blocked circulation.
“Don’t cover my rainbow legs,” he said.
Already he knew he belonged
to the sky.

The Flowers at Trader Joe's

seem to imply that paradise
is just a purchase away.
Mostly, I notice, it's the older ones
who stop to look at them closely.
A large woman in a black sweater
rests her arms on the shelf of her stomach
as she carefully considers which ones to buy.
A slight man with a face
like a desert landscape
fingers the bunches one at a time.

Meanwhile, I admire the young mothers
with their children blooming around them—
like sunflowers and lilies.
These women stride down the aisles
with purpose, sure in the knowledge
that the future is theirs.
I leave them to it.

Instead, my heart is with the old ones
who surely know by now
that whatever flowers they choose
will wilt, fade, and die
but who eagerly, still, reach out
and grasp a brightly colored bouquet
to buy.

Bed

Your dreams have seeped into my pillows,
and during the day they drowse away,
as we wait for night to come.

In the morning you make me so neat,
the sheets all tucked under and smooth
as if you could wrap all your sorrows
into one immaculate package.

But at night you come to me.
I give you back your dreams
and your sorrows. You wrap
your arms around me,
and your head sinks on my pillows
as if on the breast of the mother
you never had.

Birds

Through the thickness
of summer dusk
I've heard the cool fluid
song of the thrush.
Both question and answer
it is
three notes up,
three notes down.
What can I say?

The sound that is left
after the bubbles
of pigeon voices
have broken
against the city's
stone
is a circle.

A flock of birds
makes waterfalls
in the air:
arpeggios
of movement.

They fly
from tree to tree
as though in time
to some silent music.

I too would move
to this music
if I knew it,
if my bones were hollow enough
to sing.

Regret

Just off Highway 64 at dusk
as I hurtled by on my metaled way
with all the other rush-hour traffic,
I glimpsed a dark pond
surrounded on three sides by trees
and overhung with vines.
There a great white egret stood
neck arched,
beak poised,
waiting for that flash of silver
in dark water,
wings folded white and still
as the pages of all the books
I have never written.

Bard Owl

When I first heard the name of this owl,
with its petite beak and giant eyes,
I thought it was a troubadour
or perhaps a Shakespearean owl,
born to sing the stories of its race.

Imagine then my disillusionment
when I found I was wrong.
It was a “barred owl,”
named for the pattern of its feathers.
This is just plain wrong, I thought.

So I cling to my image
of an owl who swoops
down on silent wings,
and sings its songs
of tragedy, greed, and glory,
filling the night
with eloquent
talons and feathers
the stories of all owls,
here or dead and gone.

Sorting Through Photos

Of course, I've saved
only the very best moments—
my sweet daughter cuddling
her white rabbit,
my son standing proud
in the crotch of a giant tree
my husband installed and as always,
smiling, sitting firmly at his desk.

Much larger is the stack
of discarded ones—
photos out of focus
of someone with closed eyes,
of truncated parts of people,
or those with weird
looks on their faces.

So much like memories,
only the very best moments saved,
the rest, a much larger number,
tossed on the slag heap
of imperfect and futile attempts
to capture the ephemeral
past.

The Table

Planning my move from a house
to a retirement community,
I wanted to bring my dining room table.
"But it's too big for your apartment,"
my daughter said.
Still I held my ground,
so my table and its chairs
have come with me to my new home.

Around this table
the four of us would sit
for hours after dinner,
discussing all possible subjects
silly or profound,
teasing each other and laughing,
oblivious to anything
outside the walls of our house.

By this table
my husband stood grinning
over the Thanksgiving turkey
he'd insisted on fixing,
triumphantly wielding the carving knife
as he prepared to feed his family.

Around this table we sat,
discussing my children's woes,
my students' ignorance,
my husband's chemotherapy,
and the sorry state of the world.

Now, though most often alone,
I still have my table
with its four placemats,
keeping my past intact,
reminding me of a time
when my life was full
to overflowing.

In Line at the Drugstore

I love
the man with the potbelly
because he's wearing a red shirt that clashes with
his orange hat.
because he's buying a heating pad
that's probably to ease the back pain he has
from being so overweight.

I love
the girl
with the bare legs
because she's rummaging in her purse
for her leopard-patterned cell phone
that compensates for her naked legs.

I love
the frail old man
because he has so few items
in his large shopping cart
besides his cane.

I love
the checkout lady
because she is completely bald
and she purses her fine features
with concern that the sunglasses
I'm buying might get scratched
by the other items I'm buying.

I even love myself
because I'm so full of love
I just can't help it.

Peace

I think a kitten's sleep
is a form of prayer,
the soft pink nose
and pads of her feet,
the chin turned up to
reveal her white throat
the long tail wrapped
around her silver-gray body.
"Sleeping for storm,"
I've heard it called.

Outside may be war and famine
and unspeakable cruelties
But here and now
in this little body
is peace.

Notes to Self

Please note:
This is your cat.
He's lying on the white blanket
at the foot of your bed,
the morning sunlight shining
through his translucent ears
and glancing off the silver streak
on his side
in a way it never has before
and never will again.

Please note:
This is his pose.
His front paws are crossed,
left on top,
and his long tail curls slightly
around his back legs
in a way it never has before
and never will again.

Please note:
This is your life—
not tomorrow afternoon,
not even ten minutes ago:
NOW.

Cat Litter

I use the *New York Times*
to wrap my cat litter in.

I'm especially fond of the
"Arts and Leisure" section
with its ads for shows
I will never get to see,
its photos of doe-eyed
actresses and rugged actors.

But I like the "Style"
section too
with its stunning blondes in tight,
skimpy dresses, beautiful brides
and beaming grooms.

No one is immune,
I crush them all
to surround the soiled litter.
This gives me deep
satisfaction.

With Cats

They drape themselves about the room
like living décor—
a white fluffy paw
resting on the arm of a chair
a gray silky body spread over a bed.
With them in it,
this space comes alive.
Without them,
it is dead.

For without them,
the same coffee cup,
the barren floor,
the empty bed.

With them, one never knows—
a sudden, epic battle for territory—
a hiss and a batting paw.
or unexpected affection—
the larger one determined
to wash my whole face
with his sandpaper tongue,
the two of them spooning
in the wicker basket
or lovingly grooming each other.

If we humans keep it up long enough,
the whole world will be denuded of life—
the silent, empty ocean,
the sandy, barren land.
It will be just like my apartment
without cats.

Van Gogh in a Form of Limitation: Self-Portrait, 1887

The air, you see, had begun
to thicken like drying paint around him.
It wrinkles around his head like oil
flecked with blood the red of his beard.
From the faraway look in his eyes,
you can tell he's given up
trying to claw his way out.

Jeanne Calment, the world's oldest person
at a hundred and twenty years and some,
remembers selling him colored pencils
at her father's shop in Arles.
"He was ugly, ill-tempered, and reeked of wine,"
she said. He had a gift for art, Mme Calment for life:
"A good God has forgotten me," she says.
But clearly God did not forget Van Gogh.

For here he is in the calendar on my wall,
looking out across the no-man's land of years.
Shortly before his death, in a shop in Arles,
he failed to notice how the slanting light
fell on the glossy braid of the little girl
who held out the colored pencils he'd come to buy,
the smell of fresh air and soap
rising from the sprigged muslin of her dress.

The life of Jeanne Calment flows away
like a little river in sunlight,
soon to disappear from sight.
But good old Van Gogh is still with us—
"Mon semblable—mon frère!"

VI.
The One Who Is Coming Home

Return

Old TSE, your words
rattle around in my head
like dry seeds in a gourd.
I am a child at the gate.
Will the veiled sister pray for me?
(Behind me she walks in white and blue
her finger pressed to her lips.
We must be still to hear
the dry whisper of your will.)

I wait outside your garden
with an overwhelming question:
Will these seeds live?
Will the water from your fountain
quench my thirst?
Will the branches of your trees
hold my weight?
Will their apples satisfy my hunger?
When you hear my laughter, will you turn
even if you do not hope
and hold your arms up
so that I can climb down?

Tchaikovsky's Violin Concerto in D Major

There she is—
a slender reed
in a forest of instruments—
among the many violas,
the cellos, the bases, the horns,
even a kettle drum.

And yet from her slender body,
her slight violin,
her narrow bow,
come notes of impossible
sweetness, purity, and passion.

She wears a red dress
and seems to burn brighter
than fire,
her violin incandescent,
lighting all the other instruments,
until the whole orchestra
bursts into flame.

The Stolen Children

A response to *The New York Times* article "Ukraine's Stolen Children"

Their dark eyes are wise
in the way no children's eyes
should be.
In a twist of tragedy,
sorrow has deepened
the beauty of their
already lovely faces.

The Russians ripped the children
from the arms of their families
as if they were prizes
won at a county fair.

Mothers and grandmothers
traveled for miles
across Russia, Ukraine, or Crimea
to find and rescue their children.

But what about those still lost?

Here is a girl
with long, blonde hair
who looks like
she just stepped out
of a painting by Renoir.

Here is a boy
petting a white goose
with the same pensive
expression on its face.

Here are two girls
whose lovely eyes say,
"F—you,
No one can be trusted."

Here is the face of a little boy,
held at long last
in the arms of his mother,
eyes closed,
a gentle smile of
heaven on his face.

Yes, the children have been found,
but deep in their souls
is a place that will be lost
for the rest of their lives.

The New York Times

I used to get excited when it came,
I'd remove it from its plastic wrapper
and feel its weight heavy with promise
in my hands.

But now the news seems drearily the same—
the suffering in Gaza, Ukraine, and Sudan,
the plight of Afghan women,
the shenanigans of various politicians.

My mind refuses to stretch
to encompass so much sorrow.
And I lay down the paper,
that was so heavy in my hands.

A Clean, Well-Lighted Place

After the dreams of twisting
through black tunnels
and the random images
of ruined palaces or cities
from which there is no escape,
after the confrontation with mutants
waiting around dark corners,
the confusion of strangers
and changed family members,
after all this,
here is the diner.

Lit by early morning light,
rich with the smell
of pancakes, syrup, and sausage,
couples leaning over their breakfasts
to look at each other,
children banging their spoons
and clambering up the backs of the booths—
it waits like a mother with open arms
gathering us together
in one long, warm, and welcoming
hug.

After all the political squabbles,
the talk of government shutdowns,
oversized egos oblivious
to desperate adults and crying children,
of walls to keep everyone out,
here is the diner,

equally welcoming
to black and white,
rich and poor,
and everyone in between
to comfort and shelter,
holding us all, however briefly
together.

Four O'Clock

This is the hour
when the air grows steep
as a skyscraper.
Whatever you thought
you'd accomplished
up to now
turns out to be useless.

The world drains of meaning.
Colors bleach out to leave
your apartment looking
like a moonscape.
All your best intentions
seem to have come
to nought.

It must be time
for a beer.

Plum Pit

I love the little plums of summer,
tart and sweet as first kisses.
As my teeth puncture
the tight smooth skin,
juice bursts into my mouth
(blood of my blood)
pulp yields to my tongue
(flesh of my flesh),
but the hard pit
(not bone of my bone)
keeps itself for its own.

The Begonia

Rather than counting my blessings,
I've been more likely
To count my losses—
my mother to apathy,
my father to his new family,
my son to distance,
my husband to death.

But, of course,
There have also been gifts.
for example, from a friend,
the unexpected one of a plant,
a sort of exotic begonia
with lacy, translucent leaves.

My cats quickly recognized it
as a delicacy
and lost no time
chomping down each leaf,
leaving only
sad little knobs
along the central stem.

My first impulse was
to throw the plant away.
It was ugly, I reasoned
and just took up space.
But then I noticed
a new plant growing,
thrusting bravely through the soil
alongside the old one.

And then beside each little knob
along the main stem of the older plant,
a tiny new leaf popped out,
as if mocking my cats'
voracious appetites.

Thus my plant has taught me
I should count my losses as blessings,
spaces for new leaves
to grow from old wounds.
If only I were wise and brave
as my begonia.

Hibiscus

The eye through which I see God
is the same eye through which God sees me.
—Meister Eckhart

If this red were a sound
it would be a siren
blaring over many
loudspeakers.
Considering myself a lover of subtlety
I had not realized these flowers
would trumpet
such brazen colors.
Really, it's almost embarrassing.

Every time I pass
I gawk
like a rubberneck at an accident.
The furry red anthers of the stamen
stare back from the frothy yellow pistil
like five space-alien eyes.

No doubt, to a flower
a middle-aged woman
must look downright
exotic.

Lost Words

For the retired English teacher
it's the ultimate humiliation,
this business of noun slippage,
of lacking the *mot juste*
for any occasion.

Names are especially elusive.
"Come out, come out,
wherever you are,"
we call.
But coyly they play hide and seek
perhaps in those little folds
of gray matter,
in minds that
used to be temples
where pieces of great literature
lived their lofty lives.

Words justified
our very existence.
I speak,
therefore I am.
And if I don't speak,
do I exist at all?

The Holy Ghost

She is the ghost of a virgin.
Silent as dusty sunlight
she enters
and gathers around her the sisters
with their almost invisible lives.

(Thin the wedding veil
wrapped in tissue paper
lying at the bottom
of the cedar chest,
thin the photographs
pasted on black pages
of grandchildren's children
in distant places.
Fragile the china
locked in dusty cupboards,
fragile the bones
wrapped in weary flesh.)

In the sunlit Sunday school room
the elder church ladies gather
for coffee cake and prayers.
Discreetly cups clink on saucers.
Their murmured "Our Father"
is dry leaves falling.
"Happy Birthday to you," they sing
in voices faded as ancient flowers
pressed inside yellowed Bibles.
One by one they go.
And yet one by one they return—
gathering in the silences
as dust seems to gather in sunlight.

Deep Calls to Deep

These are your words:
the tiny iridescent blue
and yellow fish that flit
through the coral,
the small crabs that
hide themselves
in its crevices,
And even the teeth
Of the shark.

And, of course,
when I look up,
the stars that pierce
the depthless dark.

All these speak to me
in your words of light.

Kaleidoscope

For God

The world is a
kaleidoscope of colors.
From your still center
you have spun out
the earth, the trees, the skies,
the sun and moon and stars,
the wind and rain.

And we, your people
cling to the spinning
edges of your creation,
hoping
that the earth will not shift
the tides will not rise,
the sky will not cloud;
that families will not be divided,
that friends will not be lost,
that loved ones will not die;
hoping against hope
that nothing will change.

We have only to see
with penetrating eyes
through the changing seasons
of your creation
that you are still
at the center of your world.

Thank you for your stillness.
Thank you for being steadfast.
Thank you for being whole.
Thank you for
Being.

Not So Much as a Whimper

People have forgotten
how to touch each other.

Soon, they'll forget
how to talk to each other,
how to hear each other.

We are like stars in an expanding
universe, each ever farther apart.

Soon they'll be so many light years between us
we won't even be able to see each other.

And yet last night
when I looked up into the clear, cold sky,
I saw Orion stretched out plain as day against the night,
and right above me a star so bright, it seemed I could reach
up
and touch it.

Redacted

Here is the story of my life.
But look how much is missing,
Whole sentences redacted,
marked through completely
with solid black lines.
What, one wonders,
do they hide?

Could it be my not-so-little faults?
Pettiness, cowardice, greed?
Or perhaps all the acts
of which I am ashamed?
Like the time I left a scratch
on another car,
and failed to leave a note.

Or just maybe they show
what cannot be said,
the deep cravings
for all that has been
lacking in my life—
for example a strong sense of safety
from an unbroken family.

Or perhaps they simply show
how little I remember
of all the events
in my too-long life.

Left unredacted
are the mundane facts of my life.
Are even these worth preserving?
Are the redacted lines even worth deciphering?

I will never know.

Summer's End

The season is high summer,
and still the cicadas build their towers of sound.
Ah summer—
And yet just now as I walk outside,
I notice the air has cooled slightly.
The chittering of the crickets from the trees
reminds me the end of summer is coming.
And I feel strangely relieved.
I can lower my expectations
that were always high as the summer sun.
Fall will come and gently lower me down
to the leafy ground,
and though I might not be ecstatic,
I will be content.

Father of Waters

For Walt

I've been down to Bennett's Creek
to look for you.
I crouched among the laurel
and heard you speak
in the rattle of the last brown beech leaves.
I saw the river come loafing
around the bend,
the sun strike every blade of marsh grass
into fire.

Though you loafed and lounged, you were
intense as an egret's beak,
finely strung as a Stradivarius.
And the fingers of all the waters
plucked your strings,
the mouths of all the rivers
murmured your name—
Elizabeth, Lafayette, Nansemond, James.
Whether queen or commoner,
hero or slave,
you answered.
You opened your arms
and the long silver rivers flowed through you,
the wind, crazy with spring,
filled your lungs with song.

I went down into the streets
among the people you love
and listened for your voice.

I heard that the Dow was down ten points,
that I could buy one, get one free,
that sixteen Palestinians were shot by Israeli troops
(or was it the other way around?)
and someone kept shouting about Jesus.
But I never heard your voice.
So I've come back to the marshes,
where the streams are your shining arms,
reaching out to hold me,
the grass your springy hair,
breathing its heady, rank perfume,
the wind your endless voice
calling, so softly,
come home.

Janus's Daughter

For Patti Holt

In the beginning,
our father
stood looking out his doorway,
but disgusted by the chaos of creation,
he turned to stare forever
into the darkness of his house.

He wanted to keep me in.
But like a sliver of moon
I slipped past him.
And the light came laughing
after me
like a crowd of noisy children.

April Morning

I love the first stirrings
of birds in early morning,
the sleepy sounds
of their tentative chirpings—
the sky still dark,
the air slightly cool against my skin
as I slip from my bed to the shower.

This is a time like no other,
of infinite possibility.
I know the sky will brighten,
the air slowly warm with the sun.
The day will ripen until
it's full and round
as that perfect piece of fruit
in our very first garden.

About the Author

Stephanie Sugioka is a retired English professor with master's degrees in creative writing and Chinese literature and a Ph.D. in education. She has published a memoir entitled *The Hidden Stream: A Life in Prose and Verse* (Unicorn Bay Press, 2020) as well as a number of poems in literary magazines. Stephanie's father was Japanese American and her mother Anglo-European American; the multicultural nature of her experience has deeply influenced her writing. Originally from Chapel Hill, NC, she now lives in Newport News, VA.

www.ingramcontent.com/pod-product-compliance
Lightning Source LLC
LaVergne TN
LVHW090609110826
845146LV00001B/321

* 9 7 9 8 9 0 1 4 6 7 2 5 1 *